A Very Special Christmas

**Ten Christmas Favorites
for the Intermediate Pianist**

**Arranged by
JERRY RAY**

Editor: Dale Tucker
Art Design: Thais Yanes

A Very Special Christmas

What's your favorite day of the year? Think for a few minutes—you have some 365 choices. Would you choose your birthday? The day you got your driver's license? Perhaps your graduation day? A particular anniversary? The Fourth of July?

For me there's only one answer: Christmas. Christmas is the most special day of the year. Beside the inspirational significance, Christmas always brings out the very best in everyone and everything. There's loads of laughter, good food, gifts under the tree, warmth and love from family and friends plus that unique thing called music. How could anyone begin to think of celebrating Christmas without hearing "Silent Night" or "Joy to the World"? Music certainly makes Christmas something special.

And what better way to incorporate music into your holiday plans than by treating yourself and some friends to a command performance at the piano. And the ten holiday favorites found in *A Very Special Christmas* are a perfect choice. So don't be shy. Quickly volunteer to play a few numbers before all the food's gone.

You see, when you add the unique ingredients of music to a special day like December 25, you end up with *A Very Special Christmas*.

Happy Holidays!

Jerry Ray

Contents

DECK THE HALLS

TRADITIONAL WELSH CAROL
Arranged by JERRY RAY

With energy - not too fast

with pedal

Deck the Halls - 3 - 1

6

AWAY IN A MANGER

JAMES R. MURRAY
Arranged by JERRY RAY

Tenderly - with much feeling

with pedal

mp

mp

decresc.

mp

Away In a Manger - 2 - 1

Away In a Manger - 2 - 2

8va

JOY TO THE WORLD

G.F. HANDEL
Arranged by JERRY RAY

Majestically - not too fast

Joy to the World - 3 - 1

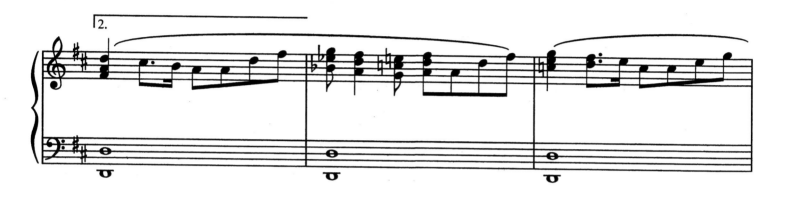

O COME, ALL YE FAITHFUL

Music by
JOHN FRANCIS WADE
Arranged by JERRY RAY

O Come, All Ye Faithful - 3 - 1

15

O Come, All Ye Faithful - 3 - 3

GO TELL IT ON THE MOUNTAIN

TRADITIONAL
Arranged by JERRY RAY

Go Tell It on the Mountain - 3 - 1

Go Tell It on the Mountain - 3 - 2

THE FIRST NOEL

TRADITIONAL
Arranged by JERRY RAY

The First Noel - 3 - 1

The First Noel - 3 - 3

SILENT NIGHT

Words and Music by
JOSEPH MOHR and
FRANZ GRUBER
Arranged by JERRY RAY

Silent Night - 2 - 1

WHAT CHILD IS THIS?

TRADITIONAL
Arranged by JERRY RAY

Moderately

What Child Is This? - 3 - 1

What Child Is This? - 3 - 2

ANGELS WE HAVE HEARD ON HIGH

TRADITIONAL
Arranged by JERRY RAY

Angels We Have Heard on High - 3 - 1

Angels We Have Heard on High - 3 - 3

WE WISH YOU A MERRY CHRISTMAS

TRADITIONAL
Arranged by JERRY RAY